Why Do We Say That (For Adults): The History and Origin of 101 Idioms, Expressions, and Sayings

Jackie Bolen

Copyright © 2023 by Jackie Bolen

All rights reserved. No part of this publication may be reproduced, distributed, or transmitted in any form or by any means, including photocopying, recording or other electronic or mechanical means without the prior written permission of the publisher, except in the case of brief quotations in critical reviews and certain other non-commercial uses permitted by copyright law. For permission requests, write to the publisher/author at the following address: Jackie Bolen: jb.business.online@gmail.com.

Table of Contents

About the Author: Jackie Bolen...6
A bee in my bonnet..7
Turn a Blind Eye..8
A dime a dozen..9
Back to square one..10
Straight from the horse's mouth..11
Beat around the bush...12
Blow off some steam...13
Caught Red-Handed..14
Crack the whip...15
Barking up the wrong tree...16
Eat Humble Pie..17
Under the weather..18
In the dog house...19
Pull out all the stops..20
At the eleventh hour..21
Caught between a rock and a hard place..22
Back to the drawing board..23
All roads lead to Rome..24
Cut to the chase...25
By the skin of his teeth..26
Got up on the wrong side of the bed...27
Make a mountain out of a molehill...28
It's not rocket science..29
In deep water...30
Go the extra mile...31
In a pickle..32
I've got my work cut out for me...33
Got a taste of his own medicine..34
Needle in a haystack..35
Get the ball rolling...36
No pain, no gain...37
Not going to fly...38
Missed the boat..39
Pick up the slack..40
Paying through the nose..41
Money to burn...42
Learn the ropes..43
Once in a blue moon..44
Step up to the plate..45
Stealing my thunder..46
The ball's in your court...47
Spill the beans...48
When it rains, it pours...49
About Face..50
The last straw..51
Through the grapevine..52
Throw in the towel..53

Idiom	Page
Alive and kicking	54
Call the shots	55
At the drop of a hat	56
Keep it under wraps	57
Hold your horses	58
Jump through hoops	59
Jump ship	60
(It's) the best thing since sliced bread	61
Let the cat out of the bag	62
Have the upper hand	63
Has the cat got your tongue?	64
Hard to swallow	65
Cry wolf	66
Go down in flames	67
Get off scot-free	68
Push (someone's) buttons	69
Monkey business	70
Sitting on the fence	71
Take a crack at (something)	72
Ripped Off	73
Fly off the handle	74
Victory lap	75
Double down	76
Everything but the kitchen sink	77
Hit the sack	78
Knuckle down	79
Throw (someone) for a loop	80
In the blink of an eye	81
Get hitched	82
Through thick and thin	83
Neck and neck	84
Couch potato	85
Take a rain check	86
Mad as a hatter	87
Lighten up	88
Cutting corners	89
Out of hand	90
Chew the fat	91
On the ball	92
A perfect storm	93
Get your act together	94
Add insult to injury	95
Can't make heads or tails of it	96
Bring home the bacon	97
It's raining cats and dogs	98
Break the ice	99
Butter someone up	100
Costs an arm and a leg	101
Riding shotgun	102
Pull someone's leg	103

Till the cows come home	104
Pass with flying colors	105
Happy as a clam	106
Sleep tight	107
Before You Go	108

About the Author: Jackie Bolen

I taught English in South Korea for 10 years to every level and type of student. I've taught every age from kindergarten kids to adults. In my spare time, you can usually find me outside surfing, biking, hiking, or snowshoeing. I now live in Vancouver, Canada.

In case you were wondering what my academic qualifications are, I hold a Master of Arts in Psychology. During my time in Korea, I completed both the Cambridge CELTA and DELTA certification programs.

I truly hope that you find this book useful. I would love it if you sent me an email with any questions or feedback that you might have.

YouTube: www.youtube.com/c/jackiebolen

Pinterest: www.pinterest.ca/eslspeaking

Facebook: www.facebook.com/eslspeaking

Email: jb.business.online@gmail.com

Have some fun learning about the history of 101 common idioms and expressions! Some of them even go back thousands of years. This book is written in, "American English."

A bee in my bonnet

Intro: Have you ever been annoyed or angry about something and you kept thinking about it, and thinking about it? You had a bee in your bonnet.

Other forms: A bee in her/his/your bonnet.

Meaning: When a person talks or focuses too much (obsesses) about something. If a bee is in your bonnet (a hat), it buzzes and might sting you; this can be like a thought, feeling, etc., that continually buzzes around your mind. Some people can ignore a bee buzzing around their head, and others can only focus on the bee.

Origin: Likely came from the earlier Scottish idiom, "A head full of bees." It was first seen in the 1500s in England and Scotland. This means that you can't think straight or clearly. Over time, the idiom and meaning changed a little bit to the current form.

Fun fact: In the 1500s, people in both England and Scotland referred to a certain kind of hat as a "bonnet." Later, people in England started calling it a cap, while people in Scotland still called it a bonnet.

Turn a Blind Eye

Intro: Have you ever ignored something? Perhaps someone said something mean to you, but you pretended not to hear them. In that case, you were turning a blind eye.

Other forms: Turned/turning a blind eye (depends on the sentence).

Meaning: To ignore something.

Origin: It comes from a British military leader, Admiral Nelson, who was blind in one eye. In the early 1800s, he received orders to stop an attack on enemy ships. He looked through a telescope with his blind eye and said that he didn't see flags telling him to stop, so he went ahead with the attack. The attack succeeded and Nelson was promoted.

Fun fact: The person who told Admiral Nelson to stop the attack ended up being fired!

A dime a dozen

Intro: Can you think of some things that are not very valuable because they're so common? "A dime a dozen" is a good way to describe them. For example, antique dishes at a garage sale. They're nice, but usually people don't want to pay money for them. Or, people who just graduated from college but don't have much work experience. They're a dime a dozen.

Other forms: None.

Meaning: Something that is very common; not of a special value. Used in a negative way.

Origin: First seen in the 1800s in the USA when you could often buy a dozen (12) things for $0.10 (a dime), for example, apples, buns, and eggs.

Fun fact: A dime a dozen used to be a positive thing—it meant you were getting a good deal. These days, it's used in a negative way to describe something without value.

Back to square one

Intro: Have you ever had to start over on something? Maybe it was a project at work. If it doesn't work out, you can say that you're back to square one.

Other forms: None.

Meaning: Starting at the beginning again.

Origin: It came from the days when people listened to soccer on the radio. Square one refers to the goal area. The commentator would often say back to square one because of all the passes back to the goaltender and free kicks when the ball goes out of bounds. It was often said with frustration because it's boring to just pass the ball back to the goaltender instead of going on the offensive and moving up the field.

Fun fact: Some people think that this idiom might come from a game like "Snakes and Ladders," where you might have to go back to the first square if you land on a snake.

Straight from the horse's mouth

Intro: Gossip is when you talk about someone behind their back. Instead, why not get the information straight from the horse's mouth? This means directly from the person involved. It's better, right?

Other forms: None.

Meaning: A way to describe information that can be trusted because it comes straight from the person involved.

Origin: Came from horse racing in England in the 1100s. Gamblers wanted to win money, so they talked to the horse trainers and people in the stables to find out the inside information about the horses. This information is straight from the horse's mouth.

Fun fact: Another theory is that it came from looking in a horse's mouth to determine its age based on the condition of the teeth.

Beat around the bush

Intro: Do you know someone who takes a long time to say what they mean? Or they don't want to talk about the real problem in a situation? These people beat around the bush—they don't speak plainly and clearly.

Other forms: Beating around the bush.

Meaning: Avoid talking about something important or not getting to the main point directly. Some people do this because they're not good communicators. Others do this because they're avoiding a difficult topic (for example, telling someone that they failed a test).

Origin: From the early 1400s. Rich men used to hire people to beat near the bushes when they went hunting to scare the birds so that they could shoot them. They beat "around" the bush and not the bush directly because it could be dangerous to hit a bee's nest, for example.

Fun fact: These days, people often use dogs that are trained instead of sticks to scare birds out of bushes when they go hunting.

Blow off some steam

Intro: What do you do if you feel stressed out about something? Maybe you have a big presentation at work coming up. Or, you feel worried about an event or sports match. You need to blow off some steam by playing video games, going outside for a hike, or hanging out with friends.

Other forms: Blowing/blew/blows off some steam (depends on the sentence)

Meaning: To release thoughts or feelings through loud talking or strong action. For example, talking or yelling loudly about something frustrating. Or, playing some video games after a tough day at work.

Origin: Comes from the early days of railroads in the 1800s. Trains had no safety valves then, so engineers would have to release or blow off steam every once in a while to prevent an explosion. If they didn't do this, the train might blow up!

Fun fact: The first train with a steam engine was seen in Wales in 1804. The steam engine was invented in 1774.

Caught Red-Handed

Intro: Have you ever done something bad (cheating on a test or stealing something) and been caught while you were doing it? You could say that you were caught red-handed.

Other forms: None.

Meaning: To be caught while in the process of doing something.

Origin: First seen in the 1400s in Scotland. There was a law that punished people who stole farm animals and killed them for food or to sell the meat. In order for the person to be convicted, they needed to still have the blood on their hands. These days, it can refer to any bad thing, not just stealing an animal.

Fun fact: There is some suggestion that this is a racist expression because it might refer to Native people. However, this likely isn't the case, and it most likely refers to farm animals.

Crack the whip

Intro: Has your boss ever had to "crack the whip" because you weren't doing what you should have been doing? Maybe you should have been working on something but you were online shopping. Or, maybe you always took too long on a lunch break.

Other forms: Cracked/cracks/cracking the whip (depends on the sentence).

Meaning: Speaking or acting in a very strict or harsh way that tries to force others to do something. Often used in a negative way with people who are lazy. However, it can also be used in a light-hearted manner among friends or people who like each other.

Origin: Related to drivers of horse-drawn carriages from the 1600s onwards who cracked their whips to get the horses to go faster. The first use of it related to people was seen in the 1800s.

Fun fact: The carriage drivers didn't actually hit the horses. They cracked the whip above the horses' heads to scare them, which made them run faster.

Barking up the wrong tree

Intro: Have you ever been blamed for something that you didn't do? Maybe your boss thought that you did a bad job on a project, but it was actually one of your coworkers. Your boss was barking up the wrong tree.

Other forms: None.

Meaning: Blaming someone for something that they didn't do.

Origin: From the 1800s in the USA where hunting dogs would bark at the base of a tree when they thought a wild animal like a raccoon was in it. They did this so that their owners could shoot it.

But, the wild animal had sometimes already escaped, which left the dogs barking at the wrong tree. Can you imagine that? A dog barking under a tree, and the owner checks the tree but there's no wild animal there.

Fun fact: How do you think the animal escaped? Can you guess? They often jumped from one tree to another.

Eat Humble Pie

Intro: Have you ever had to apologize for something bad that you did? You had to eat humble pie.

Other forms: None.

Meaning: To accept that you're wrong and apologize.

Origin: Back in the 1300s, hunting parties would go out to kill some animals to eat. These parties consisted of rich men. Once they came back home, they'd take the best cuts of meat and give the leftovers (known as numbles/umbles) to poor people who baked them into a pie. Umbles is pronounced as "humbles," which is how it came to become known as humble pie.

Fun fact: A similar expression is "Eat crow," which has the same meaning.

Under the weather

Intro: I'm sure you've felt sick before! During that time, you were under the weather.

Other forms: None.

Meaning: Not feeling well; feeling sick. Using this expression is a good way to tell someone that you're sick without going into specific details (Sorry, I can't come to work/school. I'm feeling under the weather).

However, if you tell your mom or dad that you're feeling under the weather and have to stay home from school, they'll definitely want to know the details!

Origin: Related to traveling by boat. People often become seasick when the weather is bad, and there are lots of waves. When this happens, sick people are sent below the deck (main floor) because the boat doesn't move as much below the water.

Fun fact: It used to be, "Under the weather rail." Now, it's just, "Under the weather."

In the dog house

Intro: Have you ever been in trouble for doing something bad? Maybe you said something mean to your husband or wife. Or, you stole something from someone at work, and you got in trouble with your boss. You were in the dog house.

Other forms: None.

Meaning: In trouble because of something someone has said or done.

Origin: First seen in Peter Pan in 1911 (first a play, then a movie) when the father stays in the dog's kennel (house) instead of his own bed. He does this to express how sorry he is for causing his children to be kidnapped.

Fun fact: Some people think this actually refers to the days when slaves were brought from Africa to the USA. They came over on crowded ships with very small bunk beds for sleeping. They were so uncomfortable that people called them "dog houses."

Pull out all the stops

Intro: Have you ever done all things possible to achieve something, even the very difficult things? You've pulled out all the stops!

Other forms: Pulling/pulled out all the stops (depends on the sentence).

Meaning: To use the maximum possible effort to achieve something.

Origin: A pipe organ is an old instrument that used to be found in a lot of Churches. It's similar to a piano in many ways. The knobs that control the tone and volume are known as stops. When you pull out all the stops, you're making the maximum noise possible with the instrument.

Fun fact: You can sometimes see pipe organs in sports arenas these days, especially in the NHL (National Hockey league).

At the eleventh hour

Intro: Have you ever procrastinated about something? Maybe you didn't want to finish your homework or a project at work. It's sometimes tempting to wait until the very last second to do these things. If you do, that's at the eleventh hour.

Other forms: During the eleventh hour, until the eleventh hour, in the eleventh hour.

Meaning: At the very last minute.

Origin: It's possibly from Mathew 20:9 in the Bible (the parable of the workers). In this story, each worker received a denarius (unit of currency) for a day of work, even those who started at hour 11 in a 12-hour day. In Biblical times, if someone worked for the full day (12 hours), they received 1 denarius. In the story, the people who worked only 1 hour (at the 11th hour) received the same amount of pay (1 denarius). Fair? Maybe not! What do you think?

Fun fact: The 11th hour/The Eleventh hour are quite popular names for TV shows, movies, and songs.

Caught between a rock and a hard place

Intro: Have you ever had to choose between two bad things? Maybe you have to finish a project at work, and you have to choose between working on the weekend or staying late every night for a week. If that's the case, you're caught between a rock and a hard place.

Other forms: Stuck between a rock and a hard place.

Meaning: Describes a difficult decision with two or more options that are less than ideal.

Origin: From Greek mythology. In the Odyssey, Odysseus had to pass between a treacherous whirlpool (the hard place) and a man-eating monster on a cliff (the rock).

Fun fact: Some people think this idiom came from the USA in the 1900s. It described the terrible working conditions in copper mines. Workers wanted better conditions, but the mine owners refused. The workers then had two bad choices and were caught between a rock and a hard place. Here are there two bad options:
1. Continue working under bad conditions.
2. Quit but have no money because they didn't have a job.

Back to the drawing board

Intro: Have you ever had to start over with something? It was probably frustrating! You could say that you went back to the drawing board.

Other forms: None. But, a similar saying is, "Back to square one."

Meaning: To start over after making a failed attempt at something.

Origin: From a cartoon by Peter Arno in The New Yorker magazine in 1941. The cartoon has a burning airplane with the military pilot coming down by parachute. The engineer has design plans (drawings) under his arms, and the caption says, "Well, back to the drawing board."

Fun fact: Do you know who invented the first plane? The Wright brothers made the first plane in 1903. These days, planes rarely crash unless there is terrible weather. However, during WWI (1914-1918) and WWII (1939-1945), the technology for flying was still relatively new, and pilots could encounter more problems.

All roads lead to Rome

Intro: Do you live with a partner? Do they sometimes do things differently than you? For example, washing the dishes or cleaning the bathroom. Even though it's different, the outcome, in the end is the same (clean dishes or a clean bathroom). You could say that all roads lead to Rome.

Other forms: None.

Meaning: However you do something, there will be the same outcome in the end.

Origin: This expression was seen as early as the 1100s. When the Romans were building their road system, they built all roads going to and from Rome. The system came to resemble a bicycle wheel with Rome at the center. All roads really did lead to Rome!

Fun fact: In ancient Rome, all the cities connected to Rome but not really to each other. This was by design so that the cities wouldn't be able to coordinate to overthrow the leaders in Rome.

Cut to the chase

Intro: Do you know someone who talks a lot but doesn't say that much? Maybe their stories are way too long, and you get bored before finding out the main point. You can say, "Cut to the chase!" It means to get to the main point.

Other forms: Cuts/cutting to the chase (depends on the sentence). A similar idiom is, "Stop beating around the bush."

Meaning: Used to tell someone to get to the most important thing.

Origin: Films from the early 1900s often finished with a car chase scene, which was the most exciting part of the movie. The early meaning meant to skip unnecessary dialogue and get to this more exciting part so that the audience wouldn't get bored.

Fun fact: Did you know that the first films were silent? There was no sound which means that the directors had to rely on a lot of action (like car chases), not dialogue, to keep people interested.

By the skin of his teeth

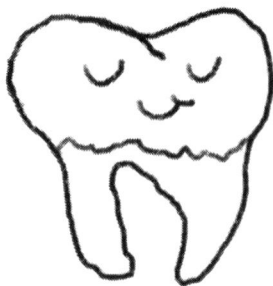

Intro: You usually need 50% to pass a test. Have you ever gotten 51 or 52%? You could say that you passed by the skin of your teeth! It was very close, and you could have easily failed.

Other forms: By the skin of her/my/our/their teeth.

Meaning: Describes doing something by the narrowest margin. For example, passing a test, escaping a bad situation, finishing a project, etc.

Origin: From Job 19:20 in the Bible: "I am nothing but skin and bones; I have escaped only by the skin of my teeth."

Fun fact: The book of Job was written around the 6th century BCE. That makes it thousands of years old! This is a very old expression.

Got up on the wrong side of the bed

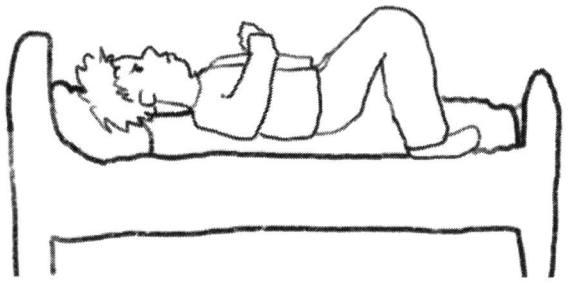

Intro: Is someone in your family grumpy when they wake up? Maybe they are a "night owl" and not a "morning person." If they're really grumpy, you could say that they got up on the wrong side of the bed. But, be careful! They might be angry at you for saying that.

Other forms: Gets/getting up on the wrong side of the bed (depends on the sentence).

Meaning: Used to describe someone who is grumpy or in a negative mood for no reason, usually in the morning.

Origin: From ancient Rome. They had a superstition that said getting up on the left side of the bed would bring them bad luck for the day.

Fun fact: In ancient Rome, which side was the good one and which side was the bad one (right or left)? Take a guess.

The right side of anything was considered to be the good side, and the left side was the bad one.

Make a mountain out of a molehill

Intro: Think about your coworkers or friends. Is there someone who makes a big deal over nothing? Maybe they make a small mistake at work, but they obsess about it for days. They are making a mountain out of a molehill.

Other forms: Making/made a mountain out of a molehill (depends on the sentence).

Meaning: Describes someone who overreacts or exaggerates about a minor problem.

Origin: This expression was seen as early as the 1500s. A molehill is a small lump of dirt made by a mole. Compared to a mountain, it's nothing!

Fun fact: "Much ado about nothing" is a similar expression.

It's not rocket science

Intro: Have you ever tried to teach someone something that is easy to do, but they couldn't figure it out? Did you feel frustrated? You could have said, "It's not rocket science!"

Other forms: It isn't rocket science.

Meaning: Describes something that shouldn't be that difficult to do, but the person is having a difficult time with it. It can be a little bit rude, so be careful about who you say it to!

Origin: First seen in 1980 as rocket science is considered to be something difficult to master.

Fun fact: Before rockets in space became popular, the expression was, "It's not brain surgery." Brain surgery is also something very difficult.

In deep water

Intro: Have you ever been in really big trouble? Maybe you broke something valuable or stole something. Or, you made a huge mistake at work. You were in deep water.

Other forms: Got/gets/getting into deep water (depends on the sentence). A similar expression is, "In hot water."

Meaning: To be in serious trouble.

Origin: From Psalm 69:14 in the Bible, ". . . out of the deep waters." Refers to someone in danger of drowning (in deep water but they can't swim).

Fun fact: Not so fun fact, but more than 320,000 people drown each year around the world. Be careful, especially when swimming in deep water!

Go the extra mile

Intro: Have you ever done something extra, more than you needed to? Maybe your friend asked you to help them move. You did that and then also helped them unpack everything. You went the extra mile! Good for you. Pat yourself on the back.

Other forms: Went/goes/going the extra mile (depends on the sentence).

Meaning: Work very hard to do a good job; doing something extra than is expected.

Origin: From Matthew 5:41 in the Bible. Under Roman law, a soldier could order a Jewish person to carry his backpack for a mile. Matthew said to carry it even further than that without complaint. This is going the extra mile.

Fun fact: Matthew 5:41 is from the famous Sermon on the Mount. This is one of Jesus' most famous teachings.

In a pickle

Intro: Have you ever been in big trouble because of something you did that couldn't be easily solved? Maybe you broke something very expensive that wasn't yours! You were in a pickle.

Other forms: None.

Meaning: Describes someone in a difficult situation that can't easily be solved.

Origin: The first use was found as early as the 1500s and originally meant to be drunk (sitting in a pickle). It later came to refer to any difficult situation.

Fun fact: You can sometimes hear this expression during a baseball game. If the runner is trapped between two bases in a "rundown," the commentators might say that the person is in a pickle.

I've got my work cut out for me

Intro: Have you ever had a really big job to do? Maybe you started a large craft project that ended up taking way longer than expected. Or, you adopted a dog with lots of behavior issues. You had your work cut out for you.

Other forms: Various other forms are possible. It depends on who you're talking about.

- They've got their work cut out for them.
- We've got our work cut out for us.
- She's got her work cut out for her.

Meaning: A big or difficult job to do.

Origin: Goes back to the 1600s. A good tailor (someone who makes clothes) would have everything cut out before starting to sew. Successful tailors would hire someone to do the cutting for them. They could just sew instead of having to cut out all the material.

Fun fact: The original version was positive—having someone cut out the material meant that the job would be easier. These days, it's more negative—there is a big task that needs to be done.

Got a taste of his own medicine

Intro: Have you ever been mean to somebody? And then they did the same thing to you later? You got a taste of your own medicine, and it probably didn't feel that good!

Other forms: Get/getting/gets a taste of her/their own medicine (depends on the sentence).

Meaning: Being treated in the same bad way he/she has treated other people.

Origin: It comes from Aesop's famous story when a man sells fake medicine to lots of people, claiming it would help them. When he gets sick, people give him his own medicine, which of course, doesn't work.

Fun fact: Aesop is a storyteller from Greece who lived around 3000 years ago. He is famous for his fables (fable = a short story with a moral lesson).

Needle in a haystack

Intro: Have you ever looked for something really small and it was almost impossible to find? Maybe it was a gift card or money in a messy bedroom! Or, a specific file hidden away in some random folder on your computer. You were looking for a needle in a haystack.

Other forms: Needle in the haystack.

Meaning: Describes something that is impossible or very difficult to find. The focus is on the negative loss of time, energy, and the stress of not finding the thing.

Origin: In ancient times, needles were made from bone or wood and looked similar to hay. This made them difficult to find in a big haystack. This expression was first seen around 1700 or 1800.

Fun fact: An earlier expression from the 1600s is, "A needle in a bottle of hay." Bottle is an old word for a bundle of hay, but it's no longer used today.

Get the ball rolling

Intro: Have you had to do something, but you weren't sure where to start? Maybe you had to write a report or clean your very messy garage, but you kept delaying because you didn't want to do it. Once you started, it probably wasn't that bad. You had to get the ball rolling and just begin.

Other forms: Got/gets/getting the ball rolling (depends on the sentence). Keep the ball rolling.

Meaning: Start something.

Origin: Comes from the 1840 presidential campaign in the USA, where William Harrison used "victory balls" that were pushed from one campaign stop to the next. These victory balls were quite large (10 feet in diameter) and were made from leather and tin. The crowd chanted, "Keep the ball rolling."

Fun fact: Another explanation is that it might be from the sport of croquet in the 1800s. Which explanation do you think is more likely?

No pain, no gain

Intro: Have you ever had to do something difficult to get a prize or reward of some kind? Maybe you had to get a part-time job in order to make some money to save up for something. Or, you trained hard for a running race and ended up winning. You went through some pain to gain something. No pain, no gain!

Other forms: None.

Meaning: The belief that suffering and hard work are required to achieve success. Often used for things like endurance sports, weight loss, or difficult exams. Achieving something difficult doesn't come easily.

Origin: Came into popular use in 1982. Jane Fonda used the saying in her popular workout videos.

Fun fact: Jane Fonda also came up with the phrase, "Feel the burn," which is still popular today. When you exercise, you might feel some pain in your muscles (the burn), but it's a good thing.

Not going to fly

Intro: Maybe you've seen a classmate or coworker try to do something, and you had a feeling that it would never work. For example, someone trying to pack way too many things into a meeting that is only 45 minutes long. It wasn't going to fly.

Other forms: Wasn't going to fly. Was never going to fly. Isn't going to fly.

Meaning: Describes something that isn't going to work or is basically impossible to do.

Origin: First seen in the late 1800s with the development of airplanes. Many designs were developed and tested before the first one worked. These earlier designs weren't going to fly.

Fun fact: The Wright brothers invented the first airplane that actually flew in 1903. Before that, traveling by hot air balloon was quite popular, especially in Europe.

Missed the boat

Intro: Did you have an opportunity to do something but didn't take advantage of it? Maybe you wanted to see a band or sports event, but the tickets were sold out by the time you checked. Or, you wanted to join a club, but you didn't sign up in time, and it was too late. You missed the boat!

Other forms: Misses/miss/missing the boat.

Meaning: Missing or failing to use an opportunity.

Origin: A common expression in England in the 1700s when boat transport was the main way to get around. To miss the boat meant that you were stuck, having to wait for the next one, missing out on opportunities.

Fun fact: This saying is very similar to, "That ship has sailed," which means that it's too late to do something.

Pick up the slack

Intro: Have you ever had to do some extra work because someone else was unable to? Maybe your husband or wife was sick, so you had to do more chores around the house. Or, you had a group project at work, but one of your coworkers was lazy and not helping. In these cases, you had to pick up the slack.

Other forms: Picked/picking/picks up the slack (depends on the sentence).

Meaning: Working harder because someone else isn't working hard enough. When someone sees that a task/action that needs doing isn't being done, they do it.

Origin: Slack means something that is too loose. It's related to working on ships where you'd have to fix a portion of a rope that hung too loosely by "picking up the slack."

Fun fact: A related expression is, "Cut some slack," which means to let someone off easily.

Paying through the nose

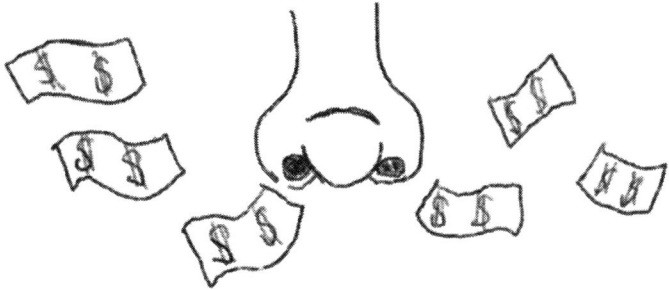

Intro: Do you have something that is very expensive? Maybe a phone, car, or designer outfit? You probably had to pay through the nose to get it!

Other forms: Pay/paid/pays through the nose (depends on the sentence).

Meaning: Paying too much or more than usual for something. For example, bottled water, food, and gas get more expensive when a big storm is coming.

Origin: It could be related to when the Danes (people from Denmark) conquered Ireland in the 800s. They took a census (official count of people) by counting noses. A large tax was imposed on each person (nose). If the person didn't pay, they'd have their nose cut.

Fun fact: The first recorded census was done around 6000 years ago by the Egyptians. They counted people, livestock, butter, honey, wool, and vegetables.

Money to burn

Intro: Do you get paid well at work? Do you like to spend it on anything that catches your eye? In this case, you have money to burn!

Other forms: None. But used positively (I have money to burn) or negatively (I don't have money to burn).

Meaning: Extra money to spend freely.

Origin: Used since the 1800s and refers to paper money that you don't need for essentials. Hence, you can afford to light it on fire and burn or waste it.

The first paper money was used in the USA in 1861. Before that, coins were used.

Fun fact: A related expression is, "Money burning a hole in your pocket." This is when someone has money that they're looking to spend. Kids might feel like this after getting birthday or Christmas money.

Learn the ropes

Intro: What's something that you learned how to do recently? Maybe it was a new hobby or sport. Or, you learned how to cook something. When you were doing this, you were learning the ropes.

Other forms: Learning/learned/learns the ropes (depends on the sentence).

Meaning: Get trained to do something. Learning how something works or how to do a task that requires specific knowledge and experience.

Origin: There are two possible explanations. The first is from people who travelled around doing rope tricks for a living. These tricks were not easy to learn and master.

The second is new sailors who had to learn to tie ropes on sailing ships. Before the steam engine, ships relied on wind power and the use of sails, which required a lot of knots.

Fun fact: In the past, a sailor would get discharge papers from the captain of the ship. If the captain wrote, "He knows the ropes," it was a negative thing. This means that the sailor is inexperienced, and only knows the basic ropes of the ship and nothing else.

Once in a blue moon

Intro: Think about something that very rarely happens. For example, maybe your boss is quite cheap. You went out for lunch with him, and he paid! You could say that it only happens once in a blue moon.

Other forms: None.

Meaning: Describes something that only happens rarely.

Origin: First seen in 1528 in an anti-Church pamphlet. The reference to the blue moon is a conversation between two people saying that if someone tells you that the moon is blue, you must believe it. The Church at that time was making outrageous statements and expecting people to believe them.

Fun fact: Another possible explanation is related to the moon cycle. Two full moons in a single month only happens every 32 months. This makes it quite rare.

The moon can also appear to be blue once in a while because of volcanic eruptions or forest fires when there is a lot of smoke and ash in the sky.

Step up to the plate

Intro: Have you ever been responsible for doing something that was a little bit difficult? Maybe your wife left you with the kids for two weeks while she went on vacation with her friends. You had to step up to the plate!

Other forms: Stepped/steps/stepping up to the plate (depends on the sentence).

Meaning: Take responsibility for getting something done in spite of it being challenging.

Origin: Comes from baseball, where the batter steps up to the home plate to hit the ball. It was first seen in the late 1800s.

Fun fact: There are lots of other expressions that come from baseball which have meanings other than during a ball game. Some of them are:
- In the ballpark.
- Hit a home run.
- To strike out.
- Touch base.

Stealing my thunder

Intro: Have you ever done something, but someone else took credit for it? Maybe you did most of the work on a project at work, but your coworker said they did most of it. They were stealing your thunder!

Other forms: Stole our thunder, stealing their thunder, steals his thunder (depends on the sentence).

Meaning: Taking credit for something that someone else did.

Origin: From the early 1700s. A playwright invented a thunder machine, and a few days later, someone stole the idea and used it in another play.

Fun fact: There are lots of other expressions that have their origins in the theater. Some of them include the following:
- Break a leg.
- Get the show on the road.
- Bravo.
- A showstopper.

The ball's in your court

 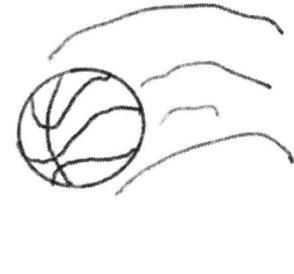

Intro: What kinds of things do you get to make decisions about? Maybe you get to decide where your family goes out for dinner. Or, what you want to do for your birthday. In these cases, the ball's in your court—the decision is completely yours!

Other forms: The ball's in my/his/her/our/their court.

Meaning: When it's someone's turn to do and/or decide something, or manage a problem.

Origin: First came into use in the 1960s from tennis. When the ball is in your court, you must hit it back to keep the point going. You have to take some action.

Fun fact: This expression was probably used to refer to other sports (basketball, for example) before becoming more general and referring to any decision.

Spill the beans

Intro: Are you good at keeping secrets? No? Then you are good at spilling the beans!

Other forms: Spilled/spills/spilling the beans (depends on the sentence).

Meaning: Tell a secret or some information. Tell something before you're supposed to.

Origin: It's thought to have originated in Ancient Greece. People used white (usually meant yes) or black/brown (usually meant no) beans to vote secretly. Then, the beans were spilled to reveal the results.

Fun fact: There are lots of other expressions related to secrets. Here are a few of them:
- Keep under wraps.
- Sweep something under the rug.
- Dish the dirt.
- Let the cat out of the bag.

When it rains, it pours

Intro: Think about a time when something has gone wrong. Did another bad thing happen at that same time? For example, your lost your job, and the family car needed an expensive repair. In that case, you could use the expression, "When it rains, it pours."

Other forms: None.

Meaning: When more than one bad thing happens at the same time, or quickly one after another.

Origin: In 1914, the Morton Salt Company was trying to find a new slogan to promote a free-flowing table salt that pours out of the box.

An old proverb, "It never rains, but it pours,"(seen as far back as the early 1700s) was found to be too negative. They ended up using, "When it rains, it pours," which was a huge success.

Fun fact: This expression was also made popular by rapper 50 Cent when he used it in a song.

About Face

Intro: Be honest! Have you ever lied about something to your boss or spouse? Did you feel bad and end up telling them the truth? You did an about face!

Other forms: None.

Meaning: A complete change of direction, either physically or in strategy. Also, when someone makes a really big change in behavior pattern.

Origin: From a long-standing military command that's thought to have originated in the British Army. In the military, it means to turn in the opposite direction.

Fun fact: There are lots of other expressions from the military that are commonly used today. Some of them are:
- On the front lines.
- No man's land.
- On the double.
- Bite the bullet.

The last straw

Intro: Maybe you've done something like this! You keep asking, and asking, and asking your boss or spouse for something, and they keep saying no. Finally, they get annoyed at you, and start yelling, and you get in big trouble! The last time you asked was the last straw.

Other forms: None

Meaning: The final annoying thing in a chain of negative things before someone finally loses their patience. For example, a child has been misbehaving all day, but his dad finally yelled at him when he wouldn't stay in his room at bedtime.

Origin: First seen in the late 1700s. Camels were often used to transport goods, and as much weight as possible was loaded onto them to get the most value from a trip. A final piece of straw was placed on the camel and caused him to collapse, breaking his back.

Fun fact: A related expression is, "The straw that broke the camel's back," which has the same meaning as this one.

Through the grapevine

Intro: How does information travel around your workplace? Do people talk at lunchtime or have a group text? When you hear some gossip, you probably hear it through the grapevine.

Other forms: None.

Meaning: To spread information informally. To hear a rumor or something that might be information through gossip.

Origin: The telegraph was invented in the USA in the 1800s. It required wire to be installed a few meters above the ground for the messages to travel along, and people thought that it looked like a grapevine. Hence, messages would travel through the grapevine.

Fun fact: This expression was made very popular by the song, "I Heard it Through the Grapevine" from 1966.

Throw in the towel

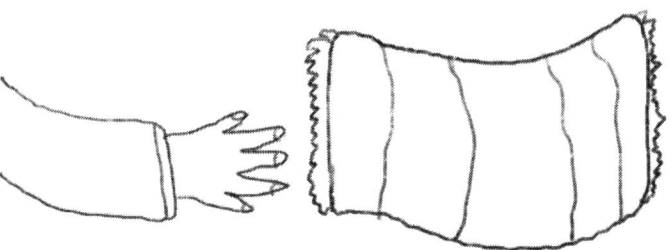

Intro: Have you ever given up on something? Maybe a puzzle or a math problem that was very difficult. Or, a club or sport that you didn't like. In those situations, you threw in the towel.

Other forms: Threw/throws/throwing in the towel (depends on the sentence).

Meaning: To quit or give up.

Origin: Comes from boxing, where a trainer throws a white towel into the ring to indicate that his fighter is giving up. This is done to protect the fighter. When the referee sees the towel, the fight has to stop.

Fun fact: This expression is closely related to raising a white flag in battle, which symbolizes surrender.

Alive and kicking

Intro: Do you know any older people who are very active, and seem like they will never die? You could say that they're alive and kicking!

Other forms: None.

Meaning: Usually refers to an older person who is still active and full of energy.

Origin: First seen in the 1800s, referring to fishermen convincing their customers of the freshness of their product. The fish is so fresh that it's still moving! It started to refer to a person who isn't dead around 1960.

Fun fact: There are lots of expressions that come from fishing. Some of them include the following:
- Big fish in a small pond.
- Plenty of fish in the sea.
- Bigger fish to fry.
- Drink like a fish.

Call the shots

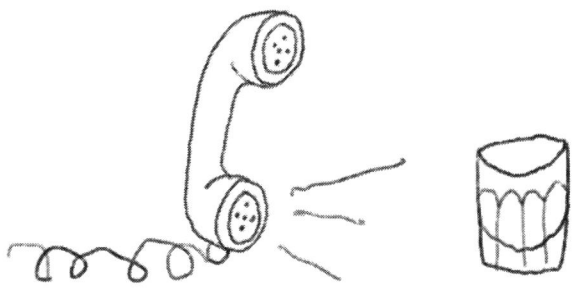

Intro: Who calls the shots at your house? This means who is in charge of the big decisions.

Other forms: Called/calling/calls the shots (depends on the sentence).

Meaning: When someone, usually an authority figure, uses their power to make decisions.

Origin: Appears to originate from the early 1900s regarding military marksmanship. An excellent marksman hits the right target and calls it his shot. When shooting animals, a good shooter will call the shot and know exactly where he or she is shooting.

Fun fact: This expression is commonly used in billiards/pool, where good players can predict which pocket the ball will go into. Bad players just shoot randomly and don't really know where the balls are going.

At the drop of a hat

Intro: Think about something that you love to do. Maybe it's playing hockey or going bike riding. What happens if someone asks you to do that with them? Do you immediately stop whatever you're doing and go do it? You did it at the drop of a hat.

Other forms: None.

Meaning: To do something without delay.

Origin: From the 1800s where dropping a hat or sweeping it in a forward motion signified the start of a race or fight.

Fun fact: It may also come from boxing. In the 1800s, at fairs, people would throw their hats into a ring to show people that they wanted to fight.

Keep it under wraps

Intro: Do you know any secrets? Did you tell them to anyone? If not, you kept them under wraps!

Other forms: Keeping/kept/keeps (something) under wraps (depends on the sentence).

Meaning: To keep something secret until a specified time.

Origin: A term from horse racing in the 1800s. It refers to a rider that intentionally keeps his or her horse from running at top speed at the beginning of the race because he or she wants people to think that the horse isn't very fast. Then, the rider lets the horse run full speed at the end to hopefully win the race.

Fun fact: During the later 1800s and early 1900s, it was used in other sports besides horse racing to describe keeping a secret. These days, it means keeping a secret in general, not just sports.

Hold your horses

Intro: Have you ever been really anxious to do something, even though someone wanted you to wait a minute? He or she might have said, "Hold your horses!" This means to wait a little bit.

Other forms: None.

Meaning: Wait a minute. Stop what you're doing or about to do, and try to be patient and think about your choice or possible action before saying/doing it.

Origin: Comes from the 1600s when people sentenced to death because of a crime were trampled by horses. The person in charge would say, "Hold your horses," and then the criminal would be tied to a piece of wood and laid on the ground. Then the horses would be released.

Fun fact: This saying could also come from the time when people used horses and wagons. You'd have to hold your horses if you didn't want the wagon to move.

Jump through hoops

Intro: Have you ever had to do a lot of steps to complete something? Maybe you wanted to join a club or sports team, and you had to fill out so much paperwork. Or, you tried to buy something online, but it was quite complicated. You had to jump through hoops.

Other forms: Jumping/jumped/jumps through hoops (depends on the sentence).

Meaning: To do a series of complicated or unnecessary things to accomplish something. They are a waste of time, but you have to do them.

Origin: Refers to circus tricks and animals that are forced by handlers to jump through hoops (at times on fire). This is often done through force by the use of whips.

Fun fact: Bend over backwards is a similar expression. However, if you bend over backwards, you're not being forced to do it—it's usually your choice.

Jump ship

Intro: Think about who you eat lunch with at work. Have you ever seen another group of people that seemed more fun? If you left to join them, you jumped ship!

Other forms: Jumping/jumps/jumped ship (depends on the sentence).

Meaning: To leave or quit something abruptly because you thought it was failing or want to go to another group/company, etc.

Origin: Refers to a sailor wishing to leave the ship without permission—thus jumping off the ship. Sailors would wait until they were close to the dock and then jump off and swim to shore. They weren't supposed to do this if they were still under contract with the shipping company.

Fun fact: This expression is often used by people who leave a company for another one.

(It's) the best thing since sliced bread

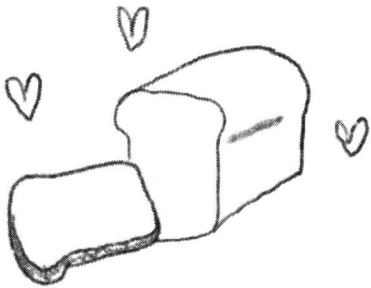

Intro: Have you recently found something new that you really love? You could maybe say that it's the best thing since sliced bread!

Other forms: "It's" = the best thing. Many possibilities.

Meaning: Something or someone that is useful or good. Refers to the best thing that has come around in a long time.

Origin: Most likely refers to a Wonderbread advertising slogan (the first company to manufacture pre-sliced, pre-wrapped bread).

Fun fact: The founder of Wonderbread was inspired by the "wonder" of hot air balloons in 1921 and gave the bread its name. Today, the company has a hot air balloon with the logo on it.

Let the cat out of the bag

Intro: Are you bad at keeping secrets? If you are, people might say, "Don't tell Jackie! She'll let the cat out of the bag."

Other forms: Letting/lets the cat out of the bag (depends on the sentence).

Meaning: To reveal a secret, on purpose or unintentionally.

Origin: First seen in the 1700s and refers to the "cat-o-nine tails." It's a whipping device (with nine cords) that is used to punish sailors. The bag refers to the leather nature of the device because it has to be stored in a bag to prevent it from drying out.

Fun fact: Another theory is that this expression is related to selling pigs. If someone bought a piglet, it was put into a bag for the person to take home. But, if the customer wasn't paying attention, the seller would put a cat in the bag instead because it isn't worth any money.

Have the upper hand

Intro: Did you have a younger brother or sister when you were growing up? Could you easily trick them into doing things for you? If yes, you had the upper hand!

Other forms: Having/has/had the upper hand (depends on the sentence).

Meaning: To have an advantage over others in a situation. Also, to be in control or a position of power in a specific kind of situation.

Origin: Refers to a way to determine teams using a baseball bat for a game. It may also refer to a couple holding hands where the dominant person has the upper hand.

Fun fact: Some similar idioms about being in a position of power include:
- Call the shots.
- Be in the saddle.
- Crack the whip.
- Hold the purse strings.

Has the cat got your tongue?

Intro: Are there some situations where you're a bit shy and don't want to talk a lot? In these situations, the cat has got your tongue.

Other forms: Not commonly seen.

Meaning: A saying to someone who is unusually quiet. Can also be used to ask why a person is not speaking.

Origin: Possibly from Egyptian times, when a person's tongue was cut off and fed to cats if the person had lied.

Fun fact: Another theory is that it's related to a fear of witches and their black cats.

Hard to swallow

Intro: Maybe you've received some news that is hard to believe or difficult to accept. Perhaps someone at work that you hate got promoted instead of you. This news might be hard to swallow.

Other forms: Difficult/tough to swallow. A difficult/tough/hard/bitter pill to swallow.

Meaning: Something that is difficult to believe or accept.

Origin: From the 1600s. It refers to pills that are sometimes hard to swallow. It originated as "bitter" (a bitter pill to swallow) and evolved to "hard" later on, but you can see lots of different forms today (hard, bitter, tough, etc.).

Fun fact: These days, drug companies are good at making small pills that don't taste that bad. In the early days of medicines, they were large and tasted terrible!

Cry wolf

Intro: Think about this situation. There's a guy at work who is always saying things that aren't true and that he needs help from the boss. Perhaps he's saying that a coworker stole things from him, but this coworker didn't actually do that. Then, someone actually steals something from that guy, and he tells the boss. What is the boss going to do? Probably not believe him! It's because he cried wolf too many times.

Other forms: Crying/cries/cried wolf (depends on the sentence).

Meaning: To call for help, ask for assistance or raise an alarm unnecessarily or when you don't need it.

Origin: From the Aesop fable named, "The Boy Who Cried Wolf."

Fun fact: This story has been around for thousands of years, and there are many variations of it. It's sometimes called, "The boy who lied," or, "A boy and false alarms."

Go down in flames

Intro: I'm sure you can think of a situation where somebody tried to do something but failed miserably. You could say that they went down in flames.

Other forms: Going/goes/went down in flames (depends on the sentence).

Meaning: To fail badly at something in an extreme manner. A similar idiom is, "Crash and burn."

Origin: From the 1940s or earlier. It's a war reference to combat planes falling to the ground, leaving a trail of fire and bursting into flames upon landing.

Fun fact: There's a similar expression, "Go _up_ in flames." This means that something is actually on fire. For example, "The apartment building went up in flames."

Get off scot-free

Intro: I'm sure that you did some bad things when you were growing up and your parents caught you. If they didn't punish you for some reason (maybe they were distracted), you got off scot-free.

Other forms: Got/gets/getting off scot-free (depends on the sentence).

Meaning: To escape punishment for something. For example, a criminal that doesn't get punished for something that he or she actually did.

Origin: It's a simple way of referring to a person not paying their taxes. It originated as "skat" (Scandinavian) and evolved to "scot" (British). It's been used since the year 1000 regarding taxes. Now it refers to anything that deserves punishment, not just avoiding taxes.

Fun fact: Another similar explanation is that some people didn't have to pay taxes on their property because it was a bad piece of land. Perhaps they had no water source, or it was very rocky. These people got off scot-free.

Push (someone's) buttons

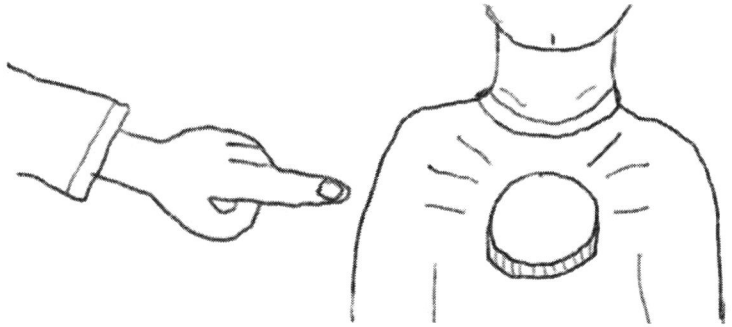

Intro: Do you know exactly what annoys your family members? Do you sometimes do it just to bug them? You are pushing their buttons.

Other forms: Pushed/pushes/pushing (someone's) buttons (depends on the sentene).

Meaning: To do something to intentionally make someone angry, upset, or frustrated

Origin: From the 1920s in the USA. Comes from a time when home appliances started requiring the push of a button to work.

Fun fact: Before the 1900s, household chores were quite difficult because of the lack of machines. You had to wash all your clothes and dishes by hand. These days, it all happens with the push of a button.

Monkey business

Intro: Did you and your siblings ever do silly or naughty things when you were growing up? You were getting into some monkey business.

Other forms: None.

Meaning: Behaving in a silly or childish manner. Mischievous activities. Can also refer to illegal or deceptive activities.

Origin: From the earlier saying, "monkeyshine," which meant dishonorable. It was from a song in 1832. Prior to that, seen in England as, "monkey tricks," used by parents to describe bad conduct in their children.

Fun fact: It may have originated in India and is seen in the Bengali language. It may have been adapted into English at a later time.

Sitting on the fence

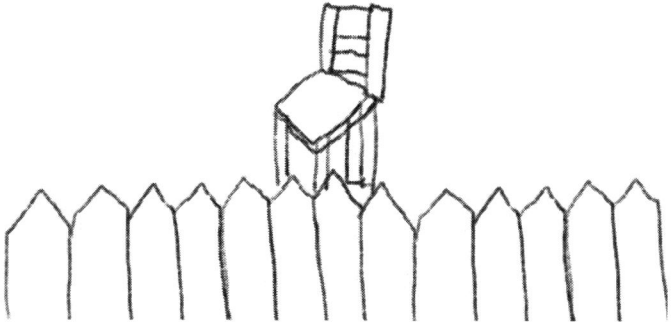

Intro: Have you ever had to make a difficult decision? If you took a long time to make it and went back and forth, you were sitting on the fence.

Other forms: Sat/sit/sits on the fence (depends on the sentence).

Meaning: When someone is trying to avoid making a choice. To not decide something until further information is presented and is convincing enough to make a decision.

Origin: In the Middle Ages, fences signified ownership of property. Someone sitting on the fence describes straddling a position between two properties.

Also has a reference to the Algonquin "Mugquomp" or "important person." It's not a term of respect but instead describes a person not making a decision as a bird on a fence.

Fun fact: You can often find this expression used in politics. It refers to someone who won't support a particular idea or person.

Take a crack at (something)

Intro: Think about something new that you've tried recently. Was it difficult to learn? When you started to figure it out, you took a crack at it.

Other forms: Took/takes/taking a crack at (something) (depends on the sentence).

Meaning: To attempt an activity that may be uncomfortable or difficult to begin at first.

Origin: Refers to the sound of a crack when a bat hits a baseball.

Fun fact: It may also come from horses and the whips that riders use. The rider cracks the whip, which startles the horse and gets them to run more quickly.

Ripped Off

Intro: Has someone ever charged you too much for something? You were ripped off!

Other forms: Rips/rip/ripping (someone) off (depends on the sentence).

Meaning: Describes when you experience someone charging too much money for something or when you are sold something that is defective or not the quality/condition you thought it was. Relates to a business transaction of some kind, usually involving money.

Origin: Rip has been used since the 1900s in the USA as prison slang for "steal." Ripped off evolved from that.

Fun fact: Musicians use this term a lot. It can refer to someone who kind of copies another artist's music (in a negative way). In a positive sense, it can be used to describe being influenced by another artist or song.

Fly off the handle

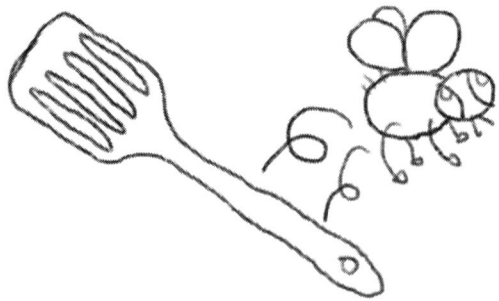

Intro: Have you ever seen someone who was really, really mad that was yelling and screaming? You could say that they flew off the handle.

Other forms: Flying/flies/flew off the handle (depends on the sentence).

Meaning: To lose control of one's emotions in a situation. Often used to refer to a boss, teacher, or parent.

Origin: Refers to the uncontrolled way in which a loose axe head flies off from its handle. It's an American saying that was first found in print in the late 1800s.

Fun fact: Think about an axe head coming off of the handle when someone is chopping wood. It can be dangerous because it's so unpredictable. It's the same with a person who is very angry.

Victory lap

Intro: Think about someone who got promoted at work. If they go around the room, getting everyone to congratulate them, they are taking a "victory lap."

Other forms: None.

Meaning: To take time to celebrate, with or without others, after a significant feat has been accomplished.

Origin: In 1988, race car driver Alan Kulwicki took an extra lap around the racetrack after winning to celebrate. Athletes in other sports do this as well, especially in running races.

Fun fact: Kulwicki died in a plane crash only a few years after doing his victory lap. Shortly afterwards, other car racers who won their races started doing "victory laps" as a way to remember him.

Double down

Intro: Think about a time that you lied about something and got caught. Did you admit your mistake or "double down" and keep trying to lie about it?

Other forms: Doubled/doubles/doubling down (depends on the sentence).

Meaning: Describe the game of poker. Doubling down is when someone doubles the amount of a bet because he or she is confident that it's going to succeed. Can also be used in a negative sense. If someone is wrong about something, instead of just admitting it, they might "double down" and do more of the same thing.

Origin: Refers to doubling your bet for a blackjack hand if you are confident that you're going to beat the dealer.

Fun fact: There are lots of expressions related to poker besides this one. Here are a few of them:
- Ace up my sleeve.
- Know when to fold.
- Dealt a bad band.
- Play your cards right.

Everything but the kitchen sink

Intro: Have you ever been camping with your family or on a road trip? How much stuff did you bring? If a lot, you could say that you brought everything but the kitchen sink!

Other forms: None.

Meaning: Everything possible, even though it's not needed or necessary. Often used to describe people with too much stuff.

Origin: It became popular in the USA during World War II, where it was often said that "everything but the kitchen sink" was thrown at the enemy.

Fun fact: An earlier idiom from the late 1800s is, "Everything but the kitchen stove." People don't use it these days.

Hit the sack

Intro: What time do you go to bed? This is when you hit the sack!

Other forms: Hits/hitting the sack (depends on the sentence).

Meaning: Go to sleep/bed. An informal saying.

Origin: May come from the times before modern mattresses. People slept on hay inside a cloth sack and had to hit it to make it more comfortable before going to sleep.

Fun fact: A similar expression is, "Hit the hay." It's from the 1800s and refers to a time when some people used to sleep in barns on hay. These days, it also refers to going to bed.

Knuckle down

Intro: When you have a big test that you need to study for, you need to knuckle down and work hard to learn the material. The same could be said for a project or report at work that needs to be done by a certain date.

Other forms: Knuckled/knuckles/knuckling down (depends on the sentence).

Meaning: To focus deeply on doing something and get to work. Usually relates to doing something difficult.

Origin: First seen in the 1800s in the game of marbles. You have to put your knuckle down to shoot the marble.

Fun fact: Another expression comes from the game of marbles, "For keeps."

Throw (someone) for a loop

Intro: Has someone ever told you something so surprising that it left you speechless? You were thrown for a loop.

Other forms: Threw/throwing/throws (someone) for a loop. (Person) was thrown for a loop.

Meaning: When something is said or done that causes a person to be surprised or shocked.

Origin: It could refer to a boxing match in which a person is struck in the head and becomes disoriented.

Fun fact: It might also refer to people riding on a rollercoaster with a loop which leaves people upside down for a short time.

In the blink of an eye

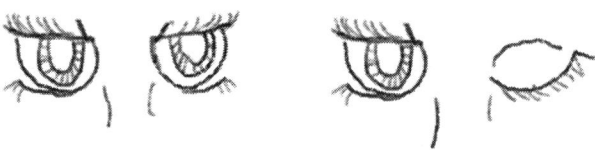

Intro: Blink your eyes. It happens so quickly, right? This expression means that something can change so fast, in the blink of an eye.

Other forms: In the twinkling of an eye (earlier version). It's used less commonly now.

Meaning: In an instant.

Origin: The earlier version (in the twinkling of an eye) is seen as early as the Bible (1 Corinthians 15:51-52).

Fun Fact: People sometimes use this expression to talk about something that happens over a longer period of time. For example, "My children grew up in the blink of an eye."

Get hitched

Intro: Think about two people you know who had a wedding recently. A funny way to say that they got married is, "They got hitched."

Other forms: Getting/gets/got hitched (depends on the sentence).

Meaning: A funny way to say get married.

Origin: From the USA in the 1500s when people used to hitch a horse to a wagon. In the 1800s, it came to refer to people who got married.

Fun fact: There are lots of expressions that mean to get married. Some of them include the following:

- Tie the knot.
- Take the plunge.
- Walk down the aisle.
- Become man and wife.

Through thick and thin

Intro: Think about two people you know who've known each other for a long time (perhaps your parents or grandparents). They've likely been through thick and thin. This means that they've been through good times and bad times together.

Other forms: None.

Meaning: To commit to something or someone despite any difficult challenges that may arise over time. Often used to describe long-lasting relationships like spouses or long-term friends.

Origin: Dates to the 1300s. It describes a forest where some areas are densely grown, whereas other areas are easy to navigate because they aren't as dense. Thick forest represents difficult times, where thin forest represents easier times.

Fun Fact: An earlier expression from hunting is, "Through thicket and thin wood." Thicket means a group of bushes that grow closely together.

Neck and neck

Intro: Think about a cycling or running race that you've seen. If the finish was very, very close, you could say that the competitors were neck and neck. It might even require checking an instant replay or photo to find out who won.

Other forms: None.

Meaning: To be even or tied in something (a competition or comparison) so that people can't tell who is ahead.

Origin: From horse racing in the 1800s, where horses are described as winning by "a neck."

Fun fact: It's not just used for sports. It can also describe politics and elections. For example, "The candidates are neck and neck leading up to voting day."

Couch potato

Intro: Think about someone who loves watching TV and hates exercise! You could say that he or she is a couch potato. Hopefully, that doesn't describe you.

Other forms: Couch potatoes (more than 1 person).

Meaning: People who aren't that active and instead prefer to sit on the couch and watch TV or play video games. Can be quite rude to describe someone like this, so be careful. However, it's fine to call yourself a "couch potato" if you really are.

Origin: From the 1970s when an American comic artist drew a comic strip with two lazy, inactive people whom he nicknamed "couch potatoes."

Fun fact: Boob tuber was an earlier expression with the same meaning, but it isn't used today. Boob tube = television. Tuber = potato.

Take a rain check

Intro: Think about a time when one of your friends wanted to hang out, but you couldn't for some reason. You could say, "Can I take a rain check?" This means that you're busy now but want to make a plan for later.

Other forms: None.

Meaning: What you can say when you can't accept an invitation at the present time, but you want to do the thing later. For example, if a friend invites me out for dinner, but I'm busy, I can say, "Can I take a rain check?" Then, we can go for dinner next week or next month.

Origin: From around 1900 from baseball. It describes people who got another ticket for a game because the one they had tickets for was rained out.

Fun fact: A rain check can also refer to a situation where someone wants to buy something at a store, but it's out of stock.

Mad as a hatter

Intro: Think about someone you know that is completely and totally crazy. You could say that they are mad as a hatter. But, don't say this directly to the person! They will be quite mad at you.

Other forms: None.

Meaning: To be completely crazy. Also, can describe someone whose behavior can be unpredictable. It's not polite to describe someone as this, so be careful!

Origin: From the 1600s when hat makers used mercury in felt hats. This resulted in people getting sick and appearing to be crazy.

Fun fact: (Not so fun fact). Mercury has been used throughout history in the process of gold mining, but it's very toxic and has resulted in a lot of deaths.

Lighten up

Intro: Do you know someone who takes everything very seriously? Maybe it's your boss or a coworker. They need to lighten up!

Other forms: None.

Meaning: Relax, chill out; don't take things so seriously. It can be a little bit rude to say this to someone as it implies that they're uptight.

Origin: From around 1400. Could be related to weighing the heart after death. If it's light (with good deeds), it goes to Heaven. If it's too heavy (with bad deeds), it goes to Hell.

Fun fact: There are lots of expressions and words that mean, "lighten up."

- hang loose
- wind down
- zone out
- chill out

Cutting corners

Intro: When someone is coming over, how do you clean your house? Do you just shove everything under your bed and in your closet? If you do, you are cutting corners. You are not properly cleaning your house.

Other forms: Cut/cuts corners (depends on the sentence).

Meaning: Choosing the least effort and lowest investment (of time, resources, etc.) when doing something. Can also refer to doing something in an illegal way.

Origin: Seen as early as the 1800s in various contexts (using an unknown shortcut when walking, metal roofers, or fox hunters trying to catch up with the dog pack by cutting corners).

Fun fact: Cutting corners, while it can save time and effort, also contains an element of risk. Maybe you'll get caught cheating. Maybe something will break and fall apart. Be careful when cutting corners!

Out of hand

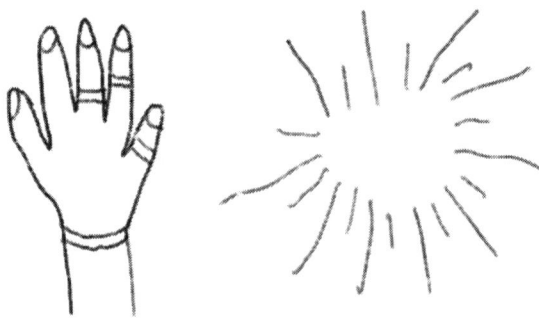

Intro: Have you ever been in a situation that got out of control? Maybe you started a small fire, and it started to get so big that you couldn't manage it. You could say that it got out of hand.

Other forms: Out of hand. Getting/gets/got out of hand (depends on the sentence).

Meaning: You're no longer able to control people or a situation.

Origin: Came from the time of wagons and horses. If the driver let go of the reins, they could lose control of the horses.

Fun fact: There's a related expression, "Rejected out of hand," which means to reject something without even considering it.

Chew the fat

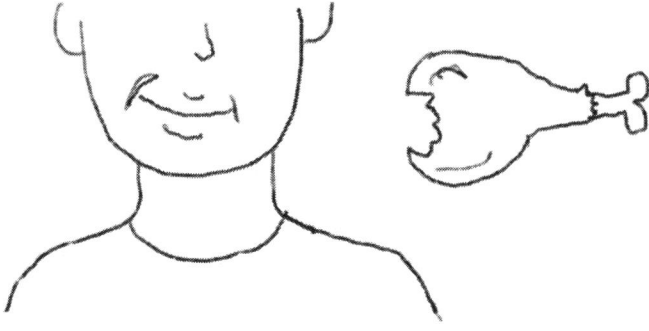

Intro: Do you know any people in your life who like to talk, and talk, and talk about not that much? They like to chew the fat.

Other forms: Chewing/chewed/chews the fat (depends on the sentence).

Meaning: To gossip or make friendly small talk in a casual, relaxed way.

Origin: From the early 1900s and could refer to sailors chewing on salted beef or pork while complaining about life. Salted beef or pork keeps for a long time without going bad, so that's why sailors would often eat it.

Fun fact: Another theory is that it refers to North American native people who would chew animal hides to make them easier to sew.

On the ball

Intro: Think about someone you know who is very organized. Maybe it's one of your coworkers or family members. You could say that they are on the ball.

Other forms: Keep your eye on the ball (means to watch something carefully).

Meaning: Indicates competence, alertness, or intelligence. Often used to describe someone who is doing well at organizing something.

Origin: Likely comes from sports and baseball specifically. You're supposed to keep your eye on the ball when hitting.

Fun fact: It may also come from cricket or golf.

A perfect storm

Intro: Think about someone who loses their job and is short on money. That's bad enough. But, then their dog gets really sick and needs to go to the vet. Then, that person's car breaks. You could say that it's a perfect storm—so many bad things happening at the same time.

Other forms: None.

Meaning: Describes a very negative situation when a lot of bad things occur at the same time.

Origin: First seen in the early 1900s to refer to the weather and boats at sea. The perfect storm means several factors that come together to produce a storm capable of sinking ships. For example, changing tides, heavy rain, and strong wind. It's used to talk about very bad situations.

Fun fact: The perfect storm is also the name of a movie from 2000.

Get your act together

Intro: Have you ever been quite lazy at work and not done a good job? Maybe you didn't get enough sleep or were hungover. Your boss might say to you, "Get your act together."

Other forms: Get/getting his/her/our/their act together (depends on the sentence).

Meaning: What you tell someone that you want to act more appropriately or be organized. Don't say this to your boss or teacher! It's better used by a parent talking to a child, for example. Also, an expression used to encourage someone to improve their performance.

Origin: Used from about 1950 onwards and is probably from the movie industry. Actors or actresses who were nervous were told to get their act together.

Fun fact: There are lots of other expressions that mean to act more appropriately.

- Pull yourself together.
- Snap out of it.
- Get a grip.

Add insult to injury

Intro: Think about a time when something bad happened to you. And then imagine another bad thing happening at that same time. You could say, "Oh no! To add insult to injury."

Other forms: None.

Meaning: Make something already bad worse. A second bad thing after an initial bad thing. For example, a guy fell off his bike, but then a car ran over his foot.

Origin: Possibly from the ancient Roman fable of a bald man and a fly. The man tried to crush a fly on his head but used too much force and hurt himself too.

Fun fact: A similar expression is, "Kick someone while they're down."

Can't make heads or tails of it

Intro: Have you ever been in class and your teacher was explaining something, but you didn't understand? You might say, "I can't make heads or tails of it."

Other forms: None.

Meaning: Unable to understand something. Can describe a work or school assignment or someone's speech or behavior.

Origin: Probably goes back to Ancient Rome. Cicero used a phrase that meant neither head nor feet to refer to confusion.

Fun fact: People in England often use the singular, "Can't make head or tail of it."

Bring home the bacon

Intro: Do you have a job that supports your family? You could say that you bring home the bacon!

Other forms: Brought/bringing/brings home the bacon (depends on the sentence).

Meaning: It is a funny way to say, "Make money with a job." This idiom is used informally (don't say this to your boss!). Less commonly, means to achieve something.

Origin: First seen in print in 1908. In 1906, Joe Gans' mother sent him a telegram telling him to "bring home the bacon" before his championship boxing match.

Fun fact: Bring home the bacon used to refer mostly to sports where it expressed the desire to win. These days, it mostly refers to money.

It's raining cats and dogs

Intro: Think about a serious rainstorm, maybe the heaviest one that you've ever been in. You could say that it was raining cats and dogs.

Other forms: None.

Meaning: It's raining a lot.

Origin: It's not entirely clear where this expression came from. However, it could be from the 1600s in Europe, where city streets often had dead animals in them. When in rained a lot, the animals were swept along the street, and you could say that it was raining cats and dogs.

Fun fact: French and old English have the word, "catadupe," which means waterfall. This phrase could possibly come from that.

Break the ice

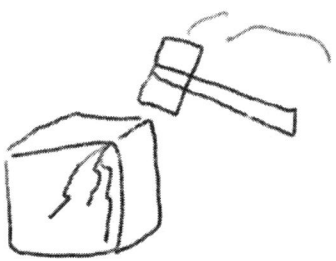

Intro: Have you ever been in an awkward situation? What did you do? If you told a joke or asked someone a question, you broke the ice.

Other forms: Broke/breaking the ice (depends on the sentence).

Meaning: To get past the awkwardness of meeting a new person.

Origin: This phrase has been used since around the 1600s to mean actually breaking through some ice, like when you go ice fishing. Later on, it meant getting over an awkward situation.

Fun fact: This is one of the most popular idioms in the English language!

Butter someone up

Intro: What do you do when you want something big from your boss? Are you extra nice to him or her for a few days? If yes, then you are buttering him or her up to get what you want!

Other forms: Buttered/buttering someone up (depends on the sentence).

Meaning: To be extra nice to someone because you want something from them.

Origin: It comes from an ancient custom in India where people threw ghee (butter) at statues of the gods in order to get some favor.

Fun fact: Ghee is actually clarified butter, which is extra delicious.

Costs an arm and a leg

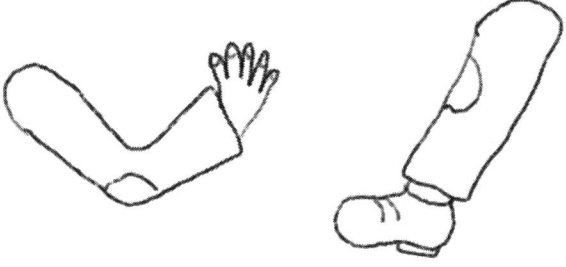

Intro: Do you have a phone, computer, or piece of sports equipment that is really expensive? You could say that it costs an arm and a leg.

Other forms: None.

Meaning: Describes something that is really expensive.

Origin: Comes from the 1600s in Ireland. Thomas ARMstrong and George LEGge manufactured the half pennies in that country, which is where it costs an arm and a leg came from. It originally referred to the Irish half penny but later came to refer to anything that is expensive.

Fun fact: This expression perhaps became more popular after WWII, when many soldiers lost arms and legs in battles. Therefore, the cost of the war was very high.

Riding shotgun

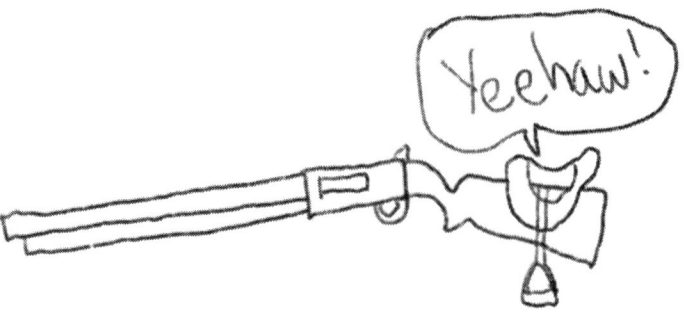

Intro: When you drive somewhere, who usually sits in the front seat next to you? That person is riding shotgun.

Other forms: Rode/ride shotgun (depends on the sentence).

Meaning: To sit in the front seat next to the driver.

Origin: In the USA in the 1700s, people often travelled in wagons pulled by horses. However, it could sometimes be dangerous as these wagons could get robbed or attacked by wild animals. Some companies started to hire a guard with a shotgun to sit next to the driver to protect the passengers.

Fun fact: If you want to sit in the front seat, make sure you are the first person to "call shotgun." This means that you claim it, and nobody else can take it from you.

Pull someone's leg

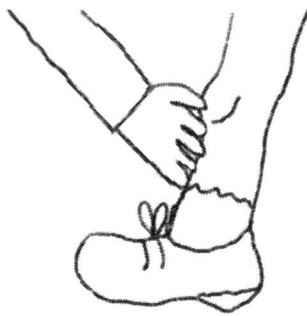

Intro: Has someone ever tricked you in a fun way? Maybe it was one of your teachers or family members playing an April Fool's joke. You could say that they pulled your leg.

Other forms: Pulled/pulling your leg (depends on the sentence).

Meaning: To trick or play a joke on someone.

Origin: It's somewhat unknown, but a theory is that thieves, who worked in pairs used to pull someone's leg to trip them, and then their partner could easily rob them. It's first seen in the late 1800s.

Fun fact: A similar expression is, "Pull the wool over someone's eyes," which means to trick someone (in a very negative way).

Till the cows come home

Intro: When you were growing up, did you ever want something from your parents, but no matter what you said, they weren't going to do it? You could argue until the cows came home, but you still weren't going to get it!

Other forms: Until the cows come home. Till the cows came home.

Meaning: A long time.

Origin: Used since the 1500s and may have come from Scotland. Cows were allowed to graze in the fields for months but would come home in the fall when there was no more grass to eat.

Fun fact: It would also refer to dairy cows who come home each morning to be milked.

Pass with flying colors

Intro: Think about a test that you did really well on. You could say that you passed with flying colors.

Other forms: Passed with flying colors.

Meaning: To pass a test by a lot (get a near perfect score).

Origin: A few hundred years ago, when ships were victorious, they put up colorful flags. When they came home, everyone would know that they had won the battle. Ships that didn't win would take down their flags. Later, it came to refer to any kind of victory.

Fun fact: A similar expression is, "Come through with flying colors."

Happy as a clam

Intro: Think about something that you really love doing. Maybe it's playing your favorite sport or watching a certain TV show. When you do these things, you are probably happy as a clam.

Other forms: None.

Meaning: Very happy.

Origin: It was first seen in the USA around 1830. When the tide is high, clams are happiest because they can't be eaten by the birds.

Fun fact: The full expression is, "Happy as a clam at high water." Today, the shorter version is used.

Sleep tight

Intro: What did your parents use to say when they were putting you to bed? If they said sleep tight, they were hoping that you slept well.

Other forms: None.

Meaning: It means, "Have a good sleep." You hope that someone is snug and cozy in bed.

Origin: It could come from thousands of years ago when people used ropes to make beds. These ropes had to be tied tightly to keep the mattress in place and provide a firm sleeping platform.

Fun fact: A similar expression is, "Sleep tight, don't let the bed bugs bite."

Before You Go

If you found this book useful, please leave a rating or review wherever you bought it. It will help other people find it! You might also want to check this out: 500+ Would You Rather Questions for Kids (by Jackie Bolen).

Printed in Great Britain
by Amazon